SONGS OF INSPIRATION

CONTENTS

— PIANO LEVEL —
EARLY INTERMEDIATE

ISBN 978-1-4768-1763-7

HAL•LEONARD®
CORPORATION

7777 W. BLUEMOUND RD. P.O. BOX 13819 MILWAUKEE, WI 53213

Visit Hal Leonard Online at
www.halleonard.com

Visit Phillip at
www.phillipkeveren.com

BLESS THE BROKEN ROAD

Words and Music by MARCUS HUMMON,
BOBBY BOYD and JEFF HANNA
Arranged by Phillip Keveren

Flowing (♩ = 60-63)

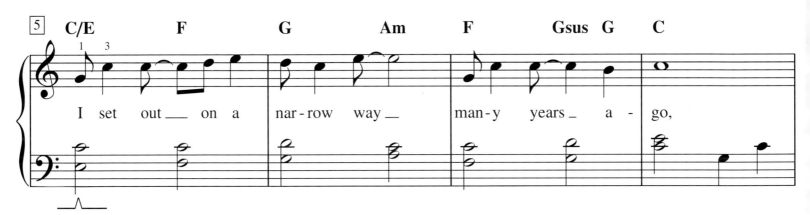

I set out ___ on a nar-row way ___ man-y years ___ a - go,

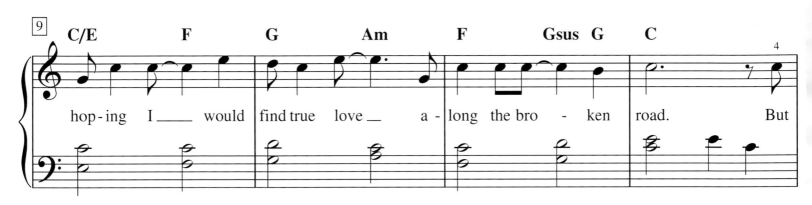

hop-ing I ___ would find true love ___ a-long the bro - ken road. But

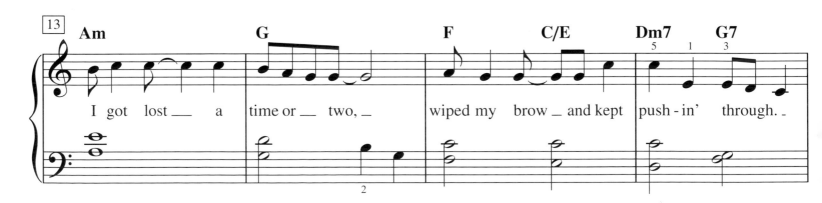

I got lost ___ a time or ___ two, ___ wiped my brow ___ and kept push-in' through. ___

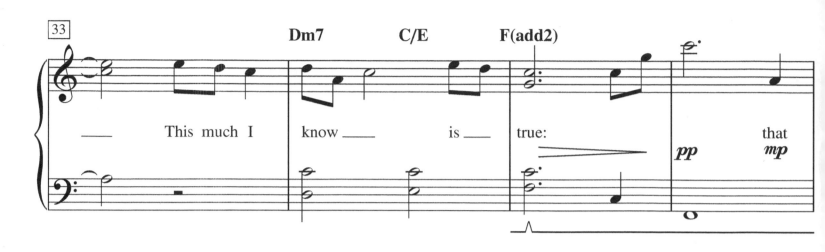

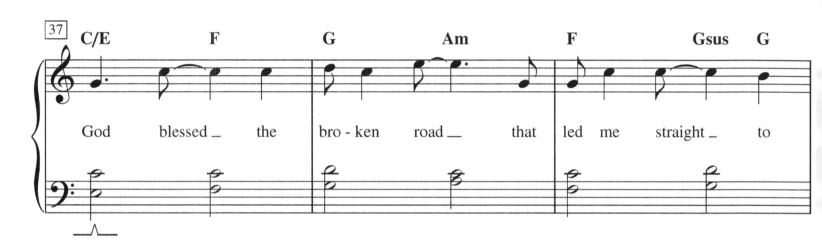

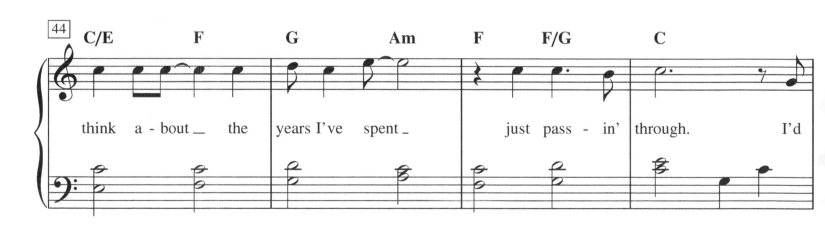

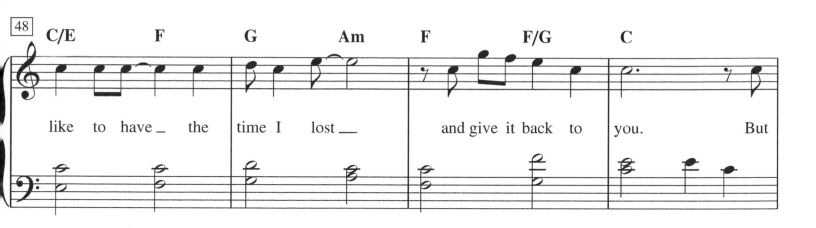

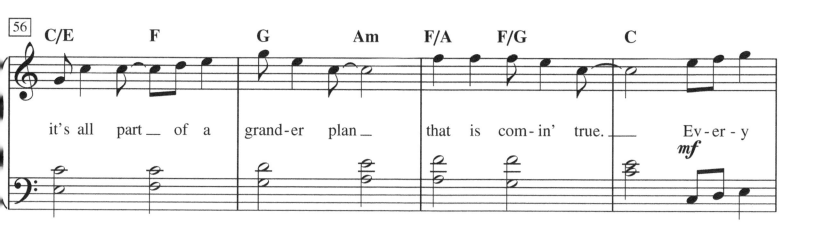

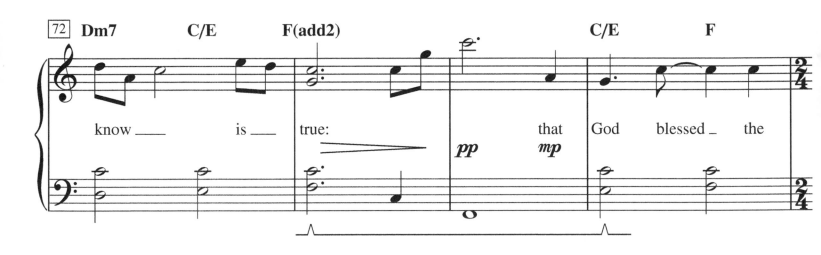

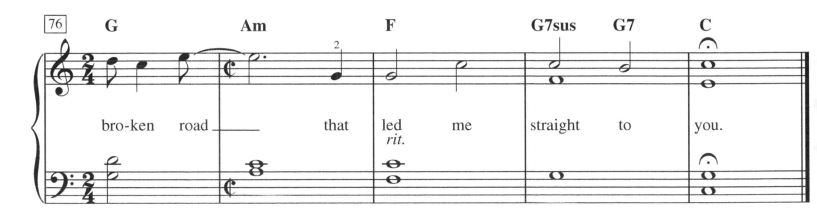

CAN'T SMILE WITHOUT YOU

Words and Music by CHRIS ARNOLD,
DAVID MARTIN and GEOFF MORROW
Arranged by Phillip Keveren

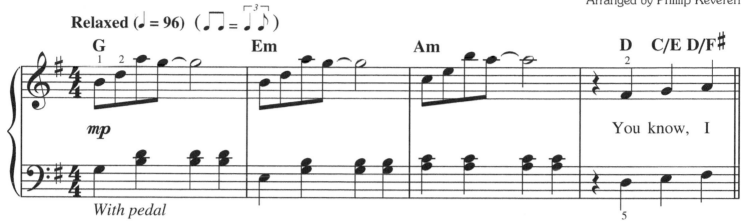

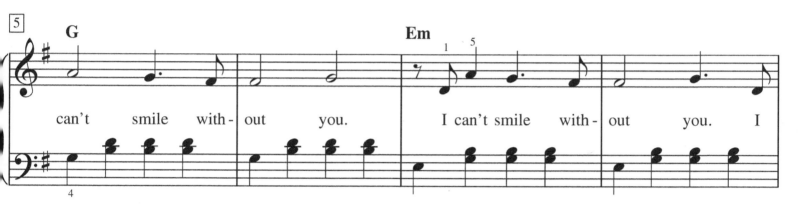

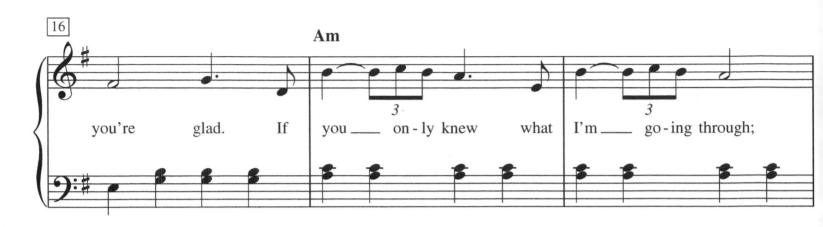

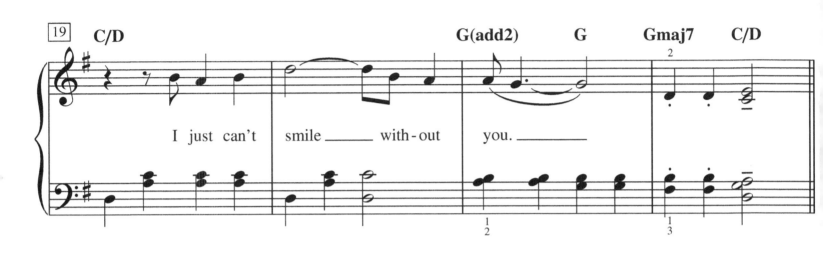

light years a - way. _ And now you know I can't smile with -

out you. I can't smile with - out you. I can't laugh _ and I

can't sing, I'm find-ing it hard _ to do an - y - thing. _ See, I

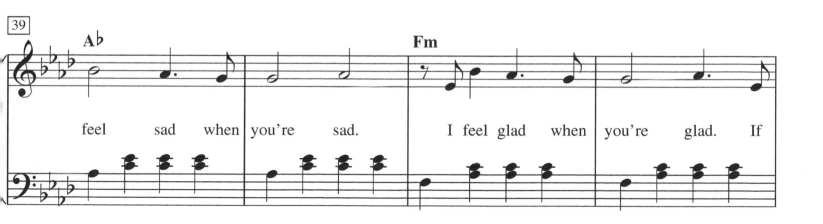

feel sad when you're sad. I feel glad when you're glad. If

you __ on-ly knew what I'm __ go-ing through; I just can't

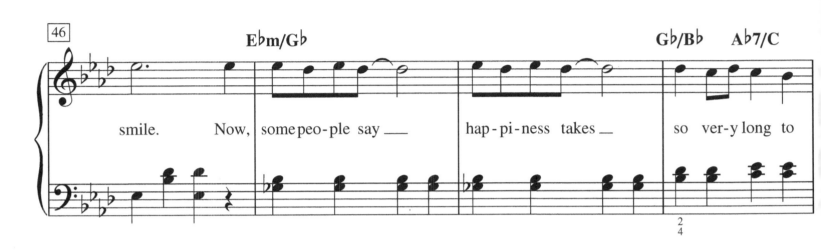

smile. Now, some peo-ple say __ hap-pi-ness takes __ so ver-y long to

find. __ Well, I'm find-ing it hard __ leav-ing your love __ be

hind me. You see, I can't smile with-out you.

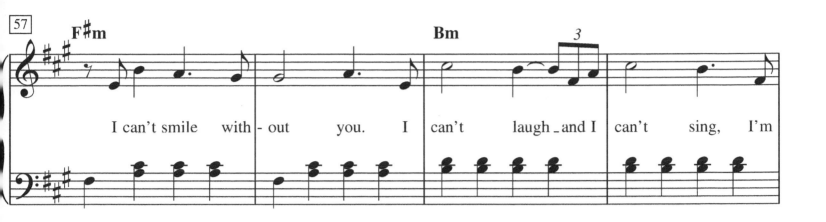

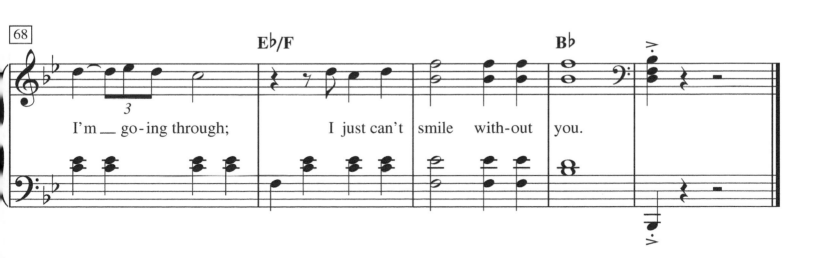

BRING ON THE RAIN

Words and Music by BILLY MONTANA
and HELEN DARLING
Arranged by Phillip Keveren

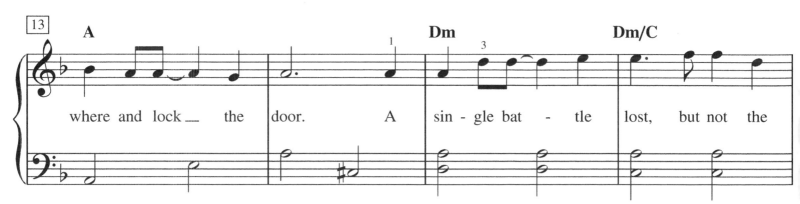

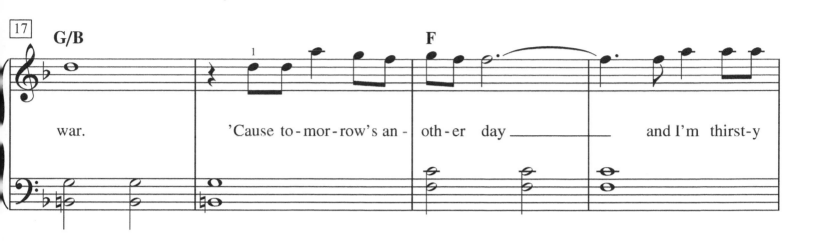

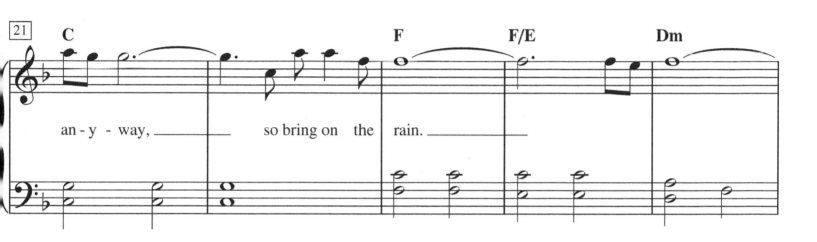

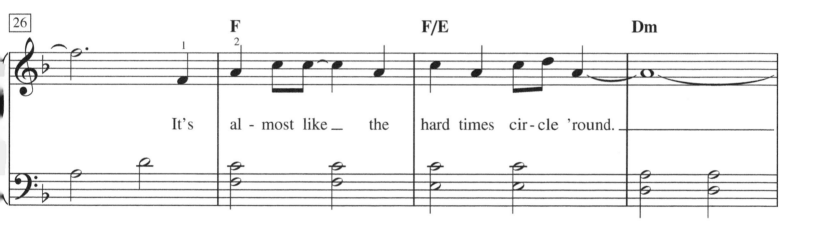

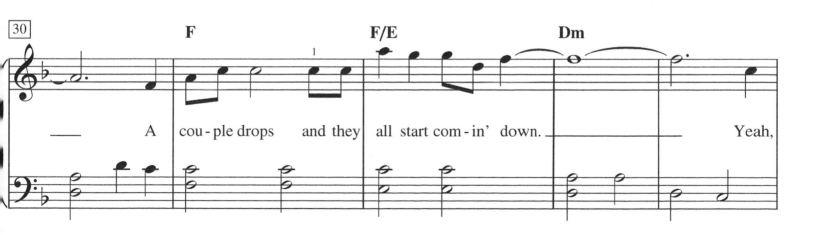

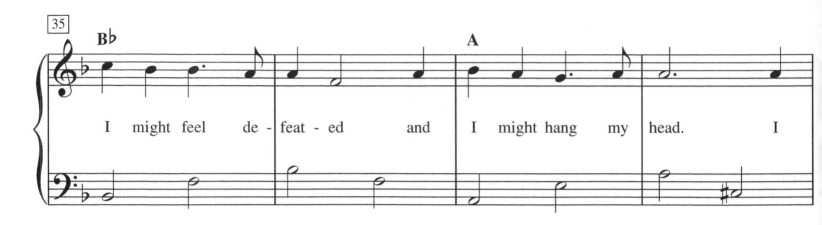

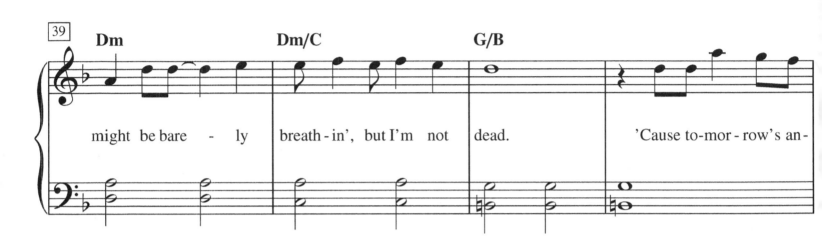

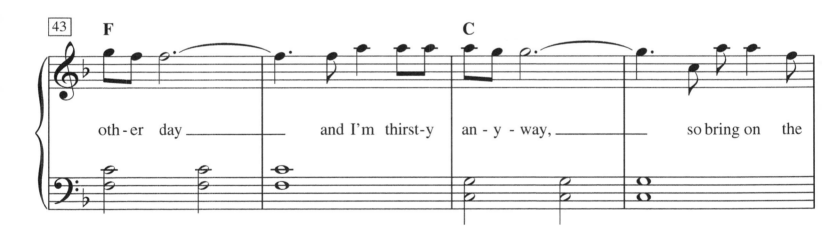

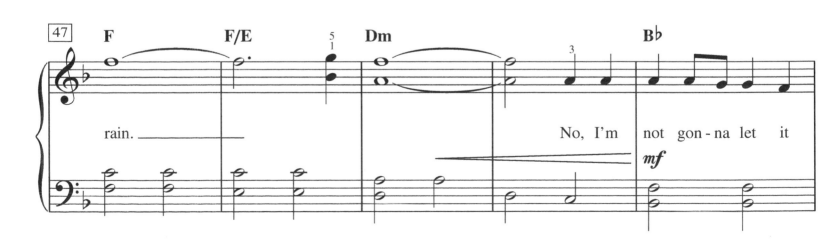

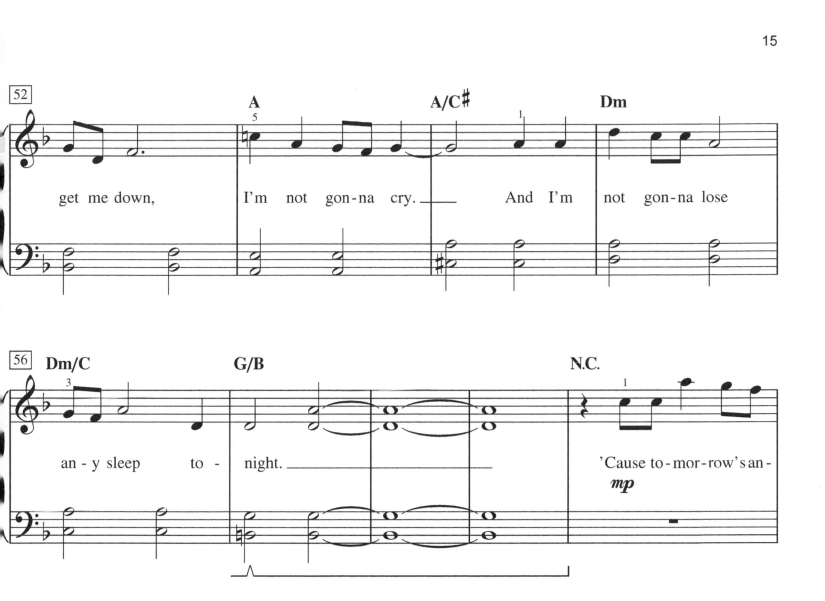

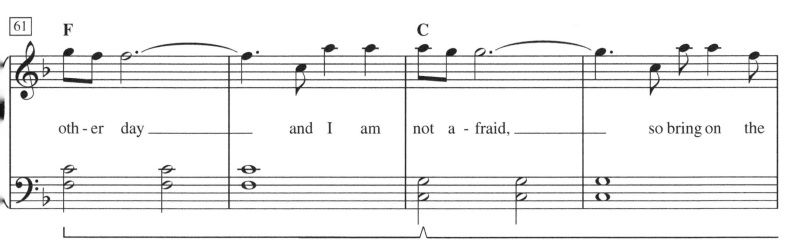

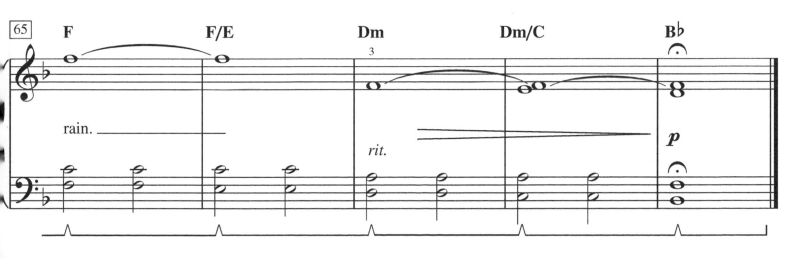

FROM A DISTANCE

Words and Music by
JULIE GOLD
Arranged by Phillip Keveren

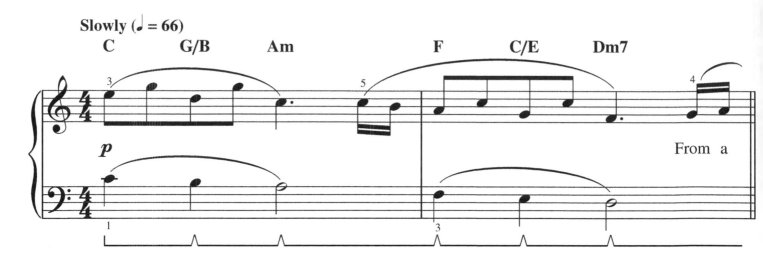

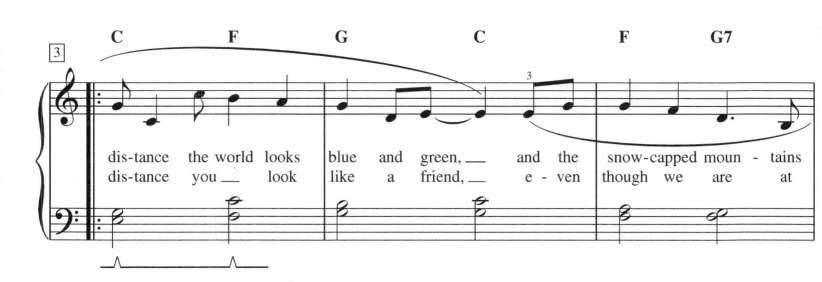

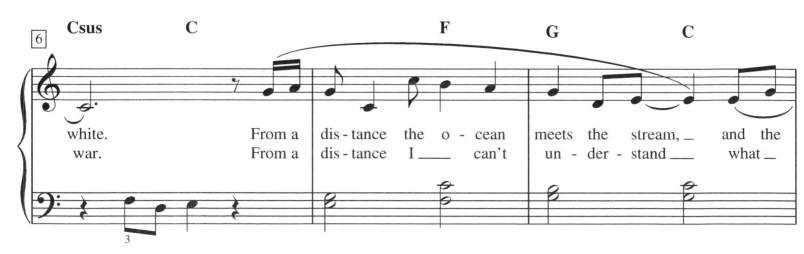

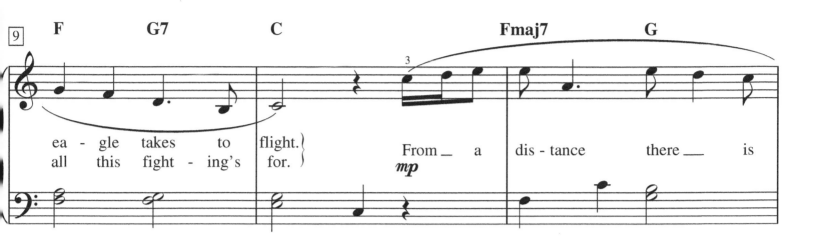

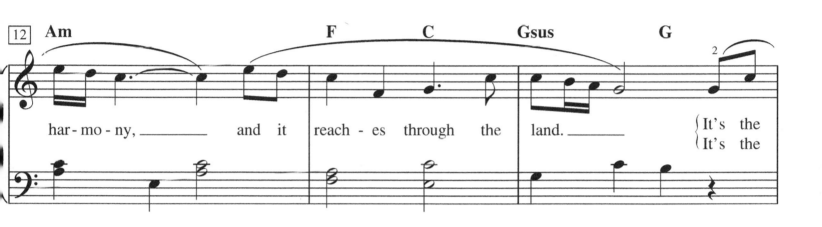

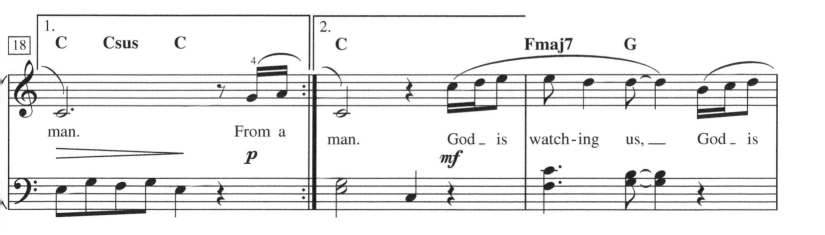

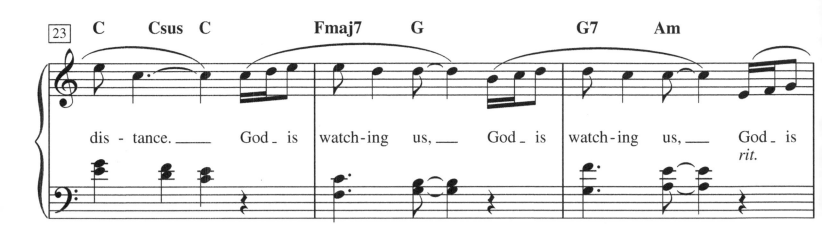

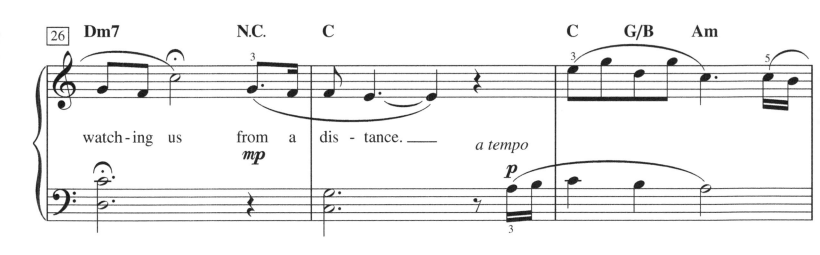

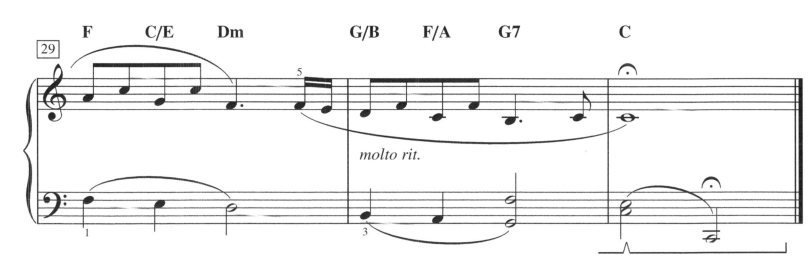

I CAN ONLY IMAGINE

Words and Music by
BART MILLARD
Arranged by Phillip Keveren

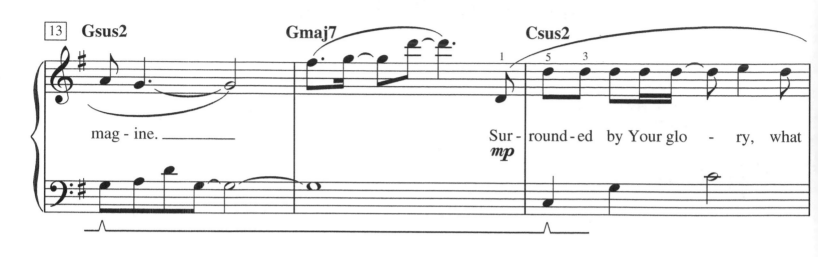

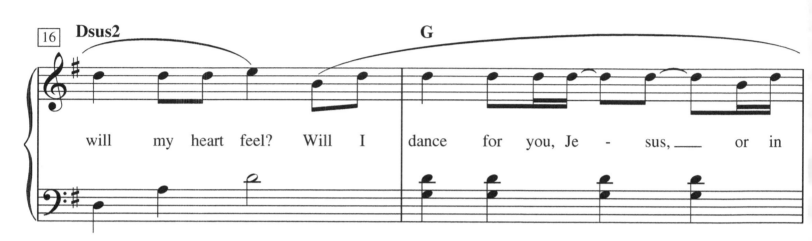

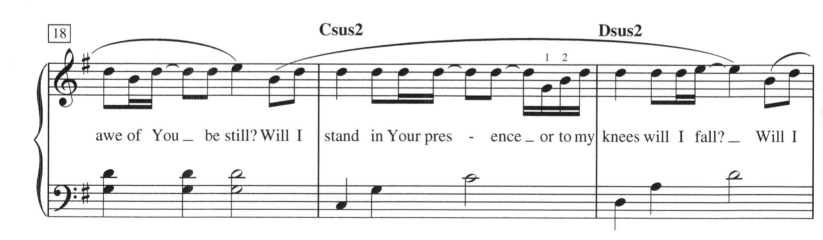

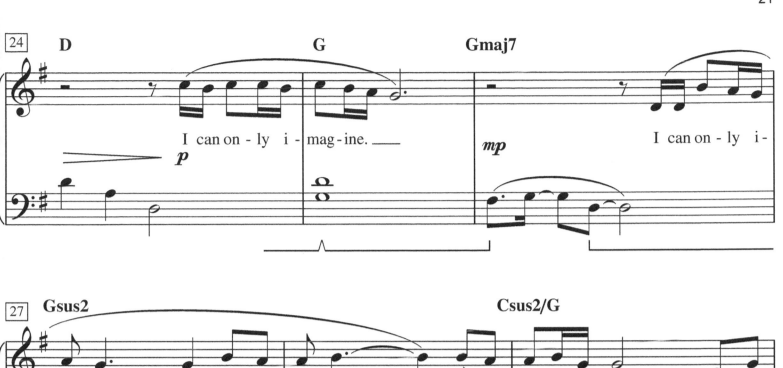

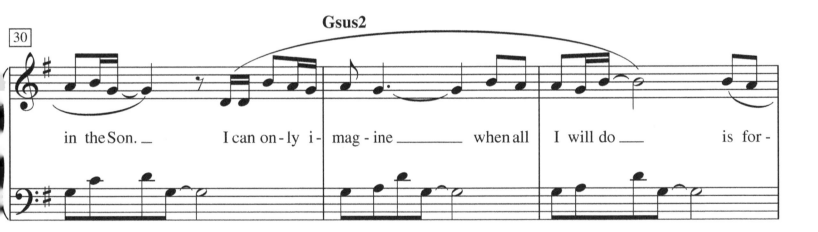

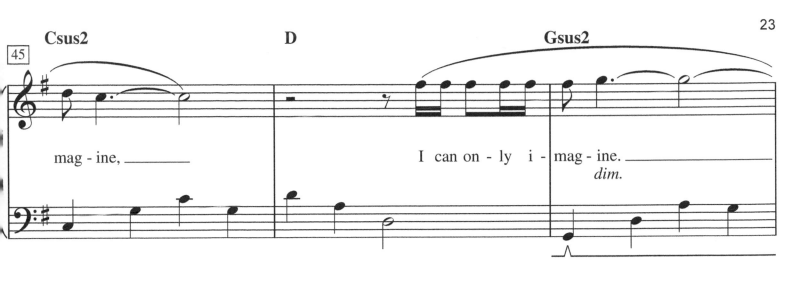

mag - ine, _____

I can on - ly i - mag - ine. _____
dim.

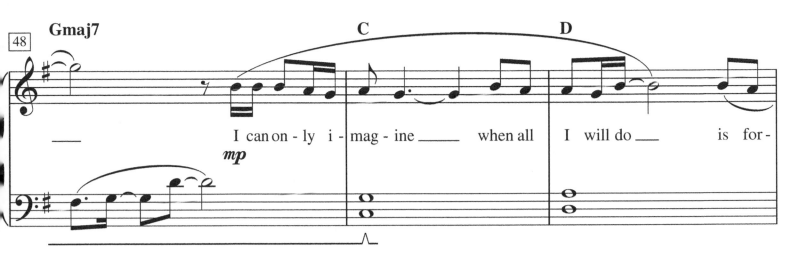

_____ I can on - ly i - mag - ine _____ when all I will do ___ is for -
mp

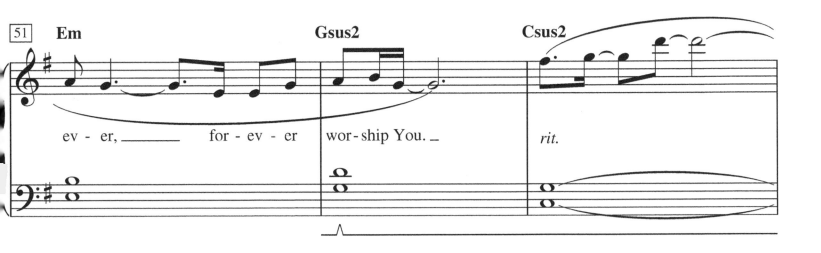

ev - er, _____ for - ev - er wor - ship You. _

rit.

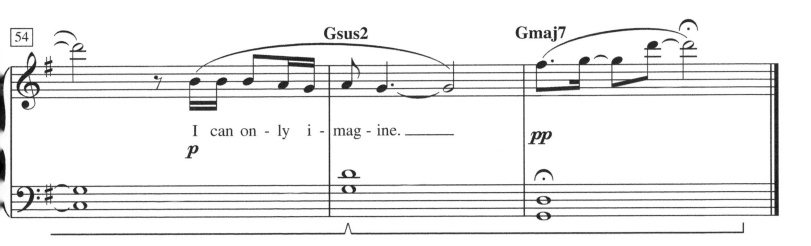

I can on - ly i - mag - ine. _____
p

pp

I HOPE YOU DANCE

Words and Music by TIA SILLERS
and MARK D. SANDERS
Arranged by Philip Keveren

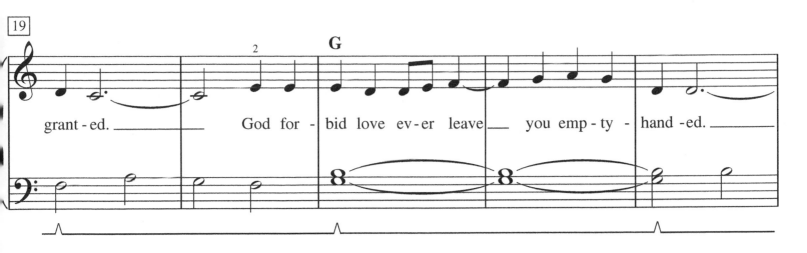

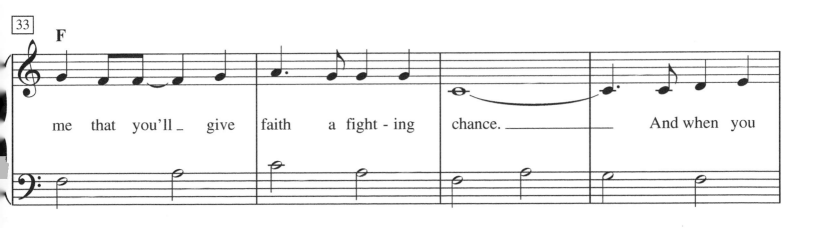

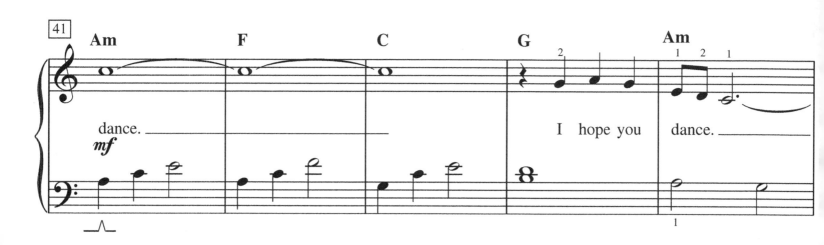

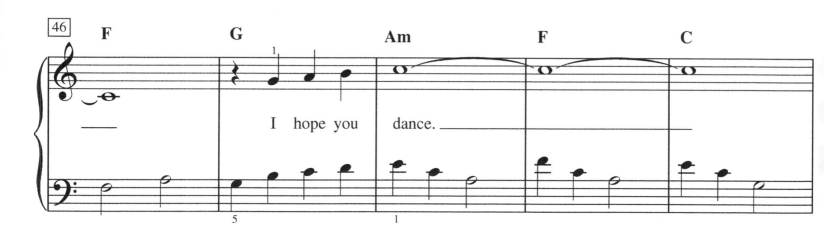

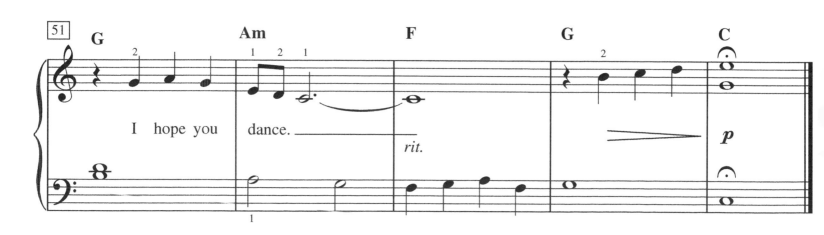

PLACE IN THIS WORLD

Words by WAYNE KIRKPATRICK and AMY GRANT
Music by MICHAEL W. SMITH
Arranged by Phillip Keveren

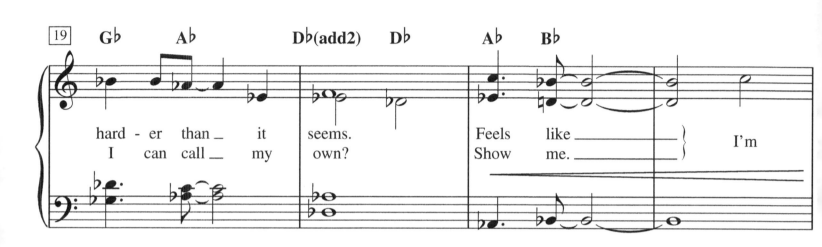

LEAN ON ME

Words and Music by
BILL WITHERS
Arranged by Phillip Keveren

Some - times in our lives, _____ we all have pain, _

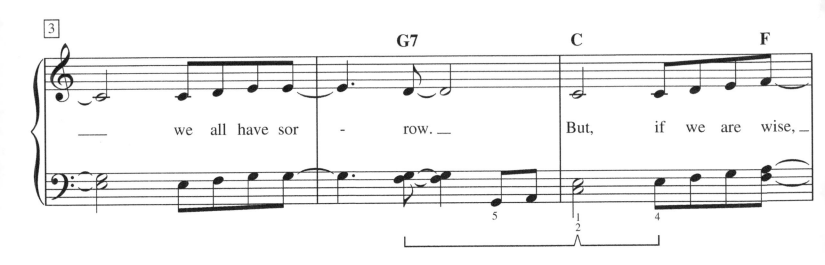

_____ we all have sor - row. _ But, if we are wise, _

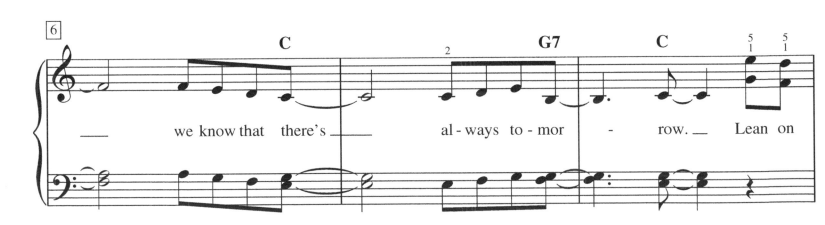

_____ we know that there's _____ al - ways to - mor - row. _ Lean on

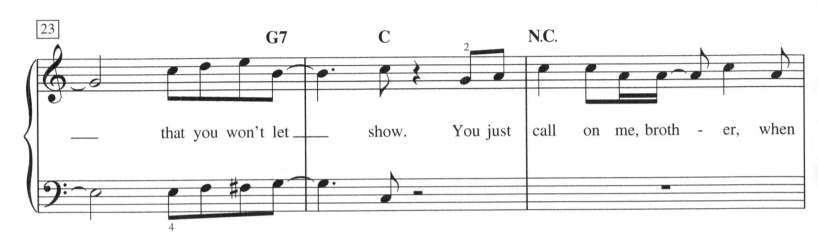

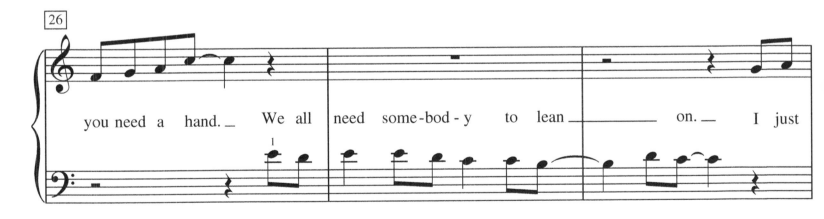

SOMEWHERE OUT THERE

from AN AMERICAN TAIL

Music by BARRY MANN and JAMES HORNER
Lyric by CYNTHIA WEIL
Arranged by Phillip Keveren

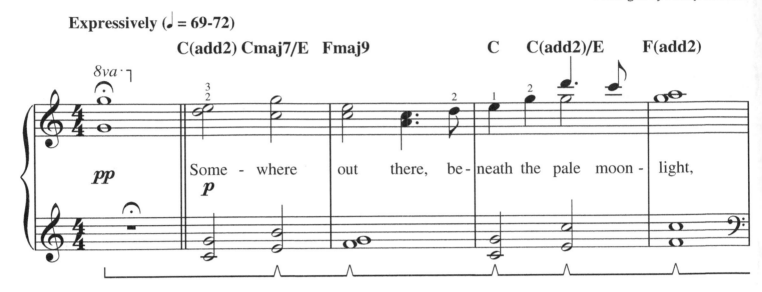

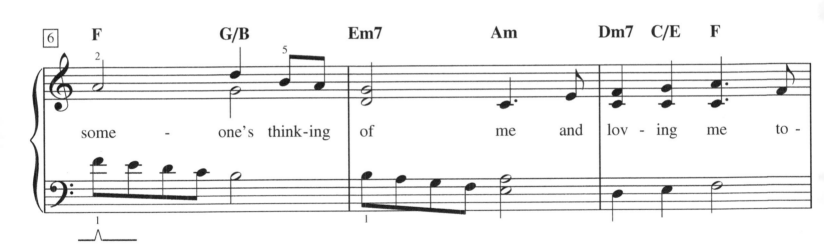

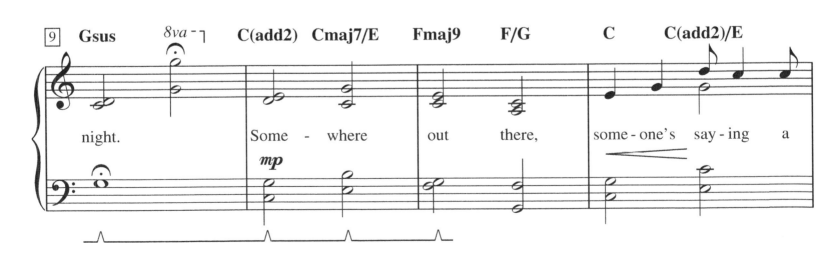

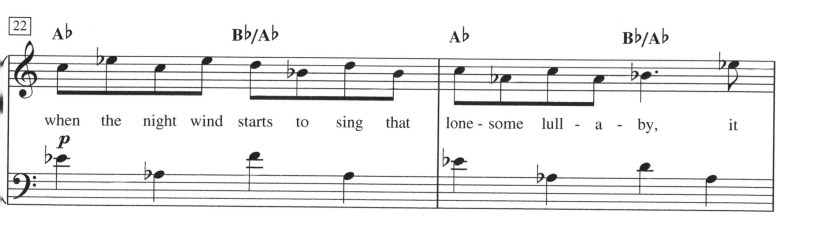

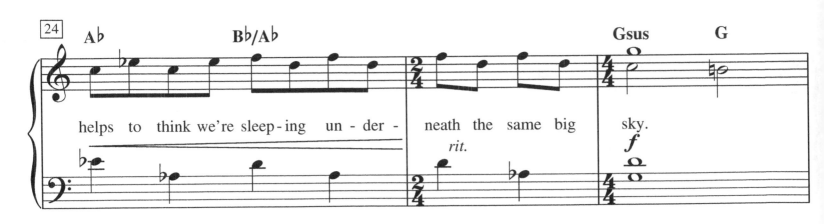

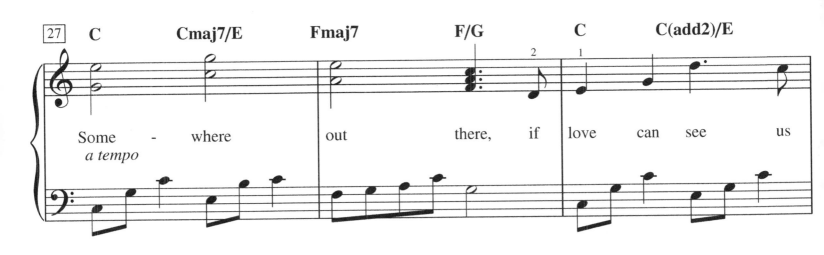

WHAT A WONDERFUL WORLD

Words and Music by GEORGE DAVID WEISS
and BOB THIELE
Arranged by Phillip Keveren

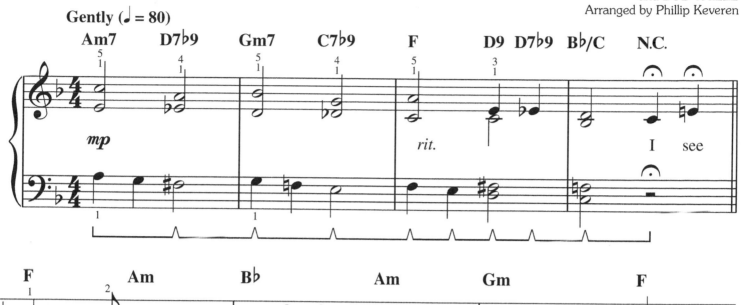

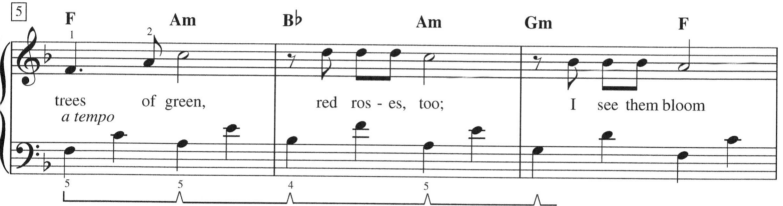

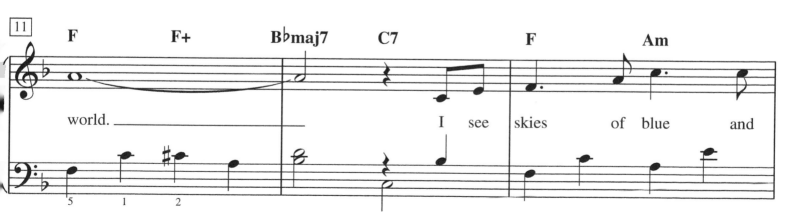

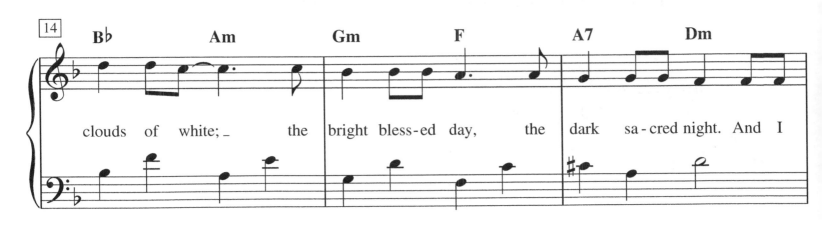

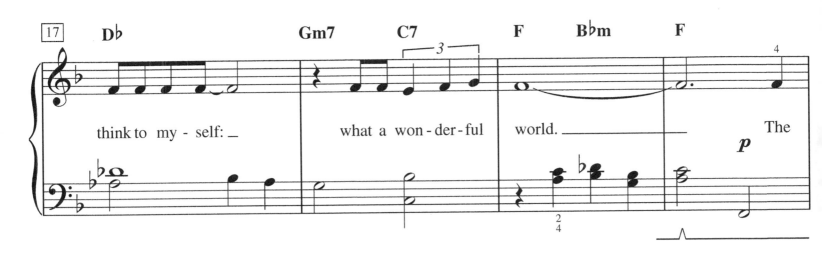

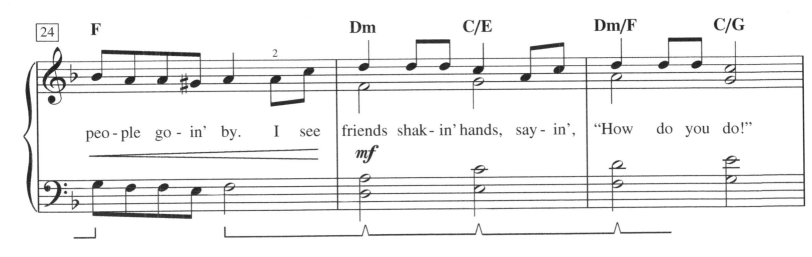

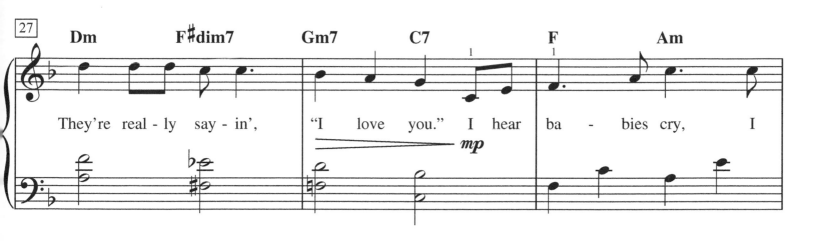

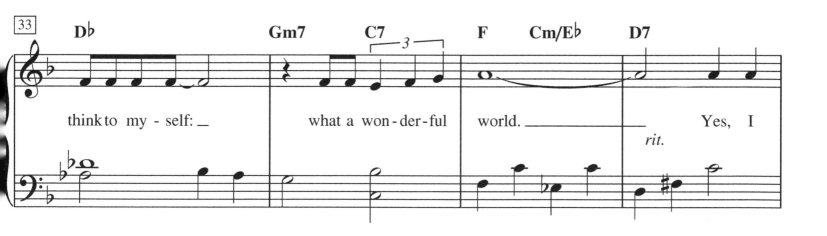

WHERE WERE YOU
(When the World Stopped Turning)

Words and Music by
ALAN JACKSON
Arranged by Phillip Keveren

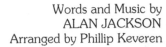

Where were you when the world ___ stopped turn - in'

that Sep-tem-ber day? Out in the yard ___ with your wife and chil-dren or

work-in' on some stage in L. A.? Did you stand there in shock at the sight of the black smoke

ris - in' a-gainst that blue sky? Did you shout out in an - ger in fear for your neigh-bor, or

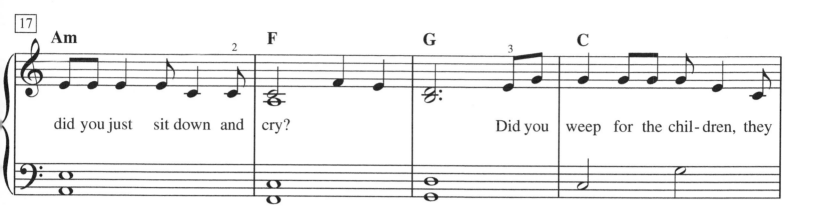

did you just sit down and cry? Did you weep for the chil-dren, they

lost their dear loved ones, pray for the ones who don't know? Did you re-

joice for the peo-ple who walked from the rub-ble and sob for the ones left be-

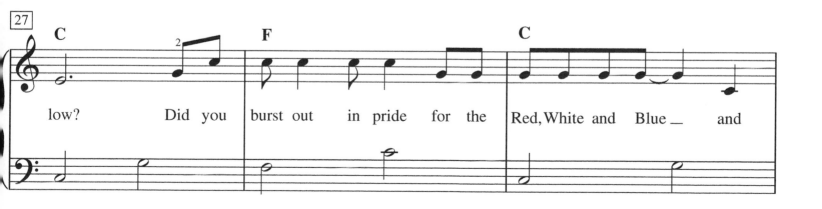

low? Did you burst out in pride for the Red, White and Blue __ and

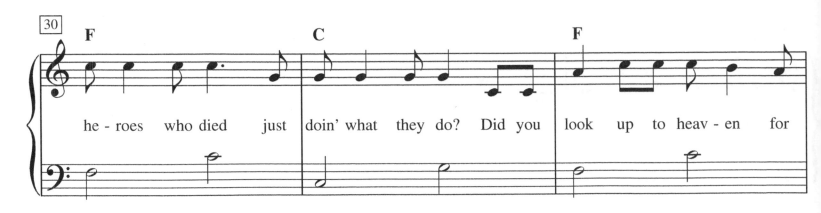

30
F
C
F

he - roes who died just doin' what they do? Did you look up to heav - en for

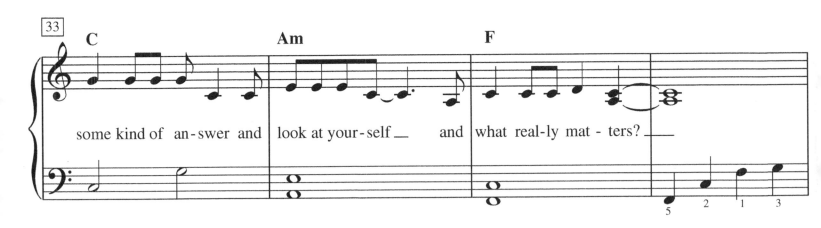

33
C
Am
F

some kind of an - swer and look at your - self ___ and what real - ly mat - ters? ___

37

I'm just a sing - er of sim - ple songs. ___ I'm not a real po - lit - i - cal

40
C
F
C

man. I watch C - N - N, ___ but I'm not sure I can tell you the

dif-f'rence in I-raq and I-ran. But I know Je - sus and I talk to God, and I re-

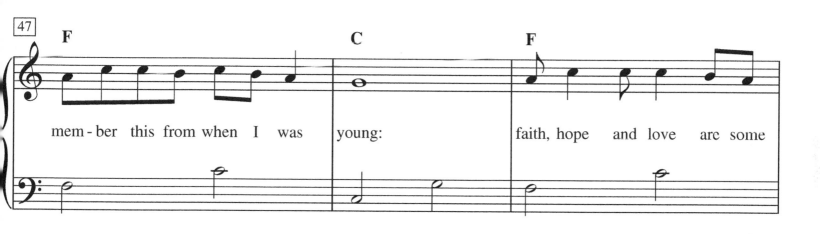

mem-ber this from when I was young: faith, hope and love are some

good things He gave us, and the great-est is love. *rit.* *p*

Where were you when the world ___ stopped turn-in' that Sep-tem-ber day?

THE WIND BENEATH MY WINGS

from the Original Motion Picture BEACHES

Words and Music by LARRY HENLEY
and JEFF SILBAR
Arranged by Phillip Keveren

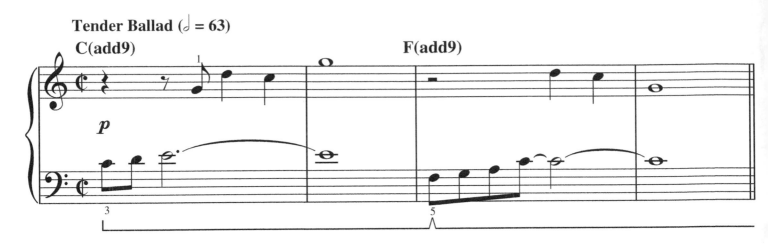

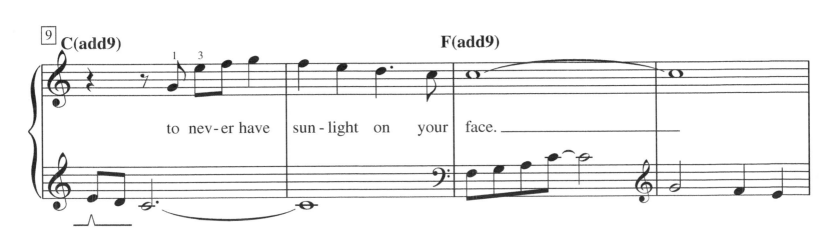

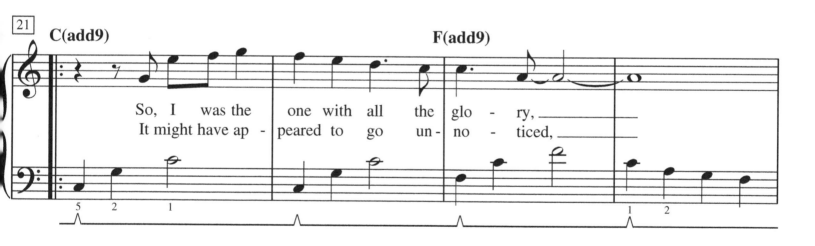

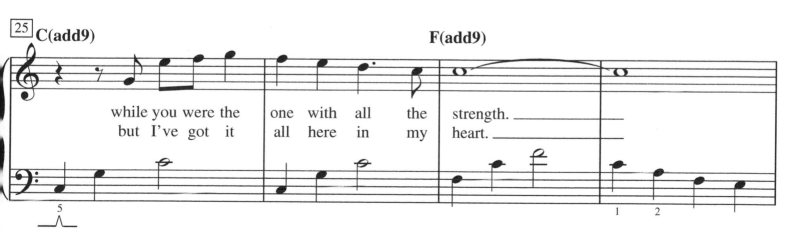

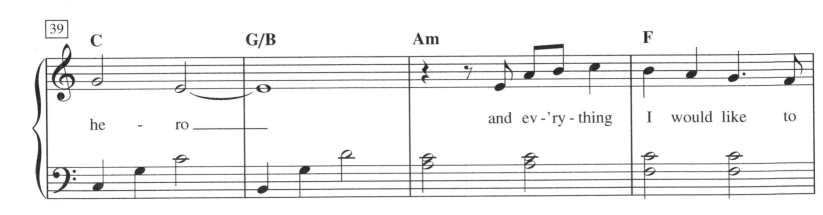

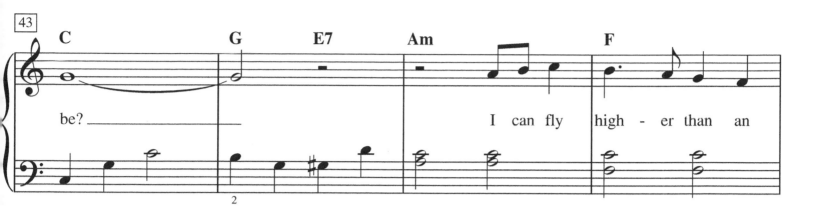

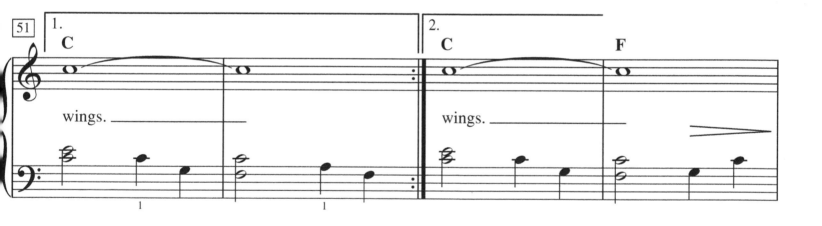

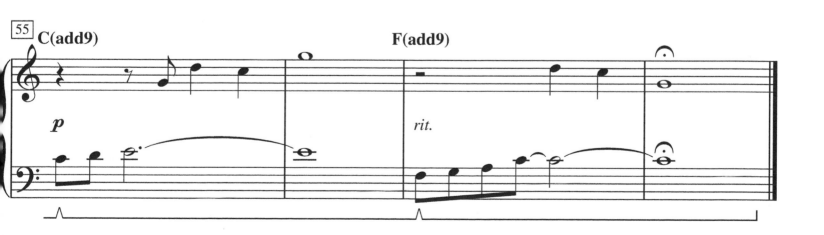

YOU LIGHT UP MY LIFE

Words and Music by
JOSEPH BROOKS
Arranged by Phillip Keveren

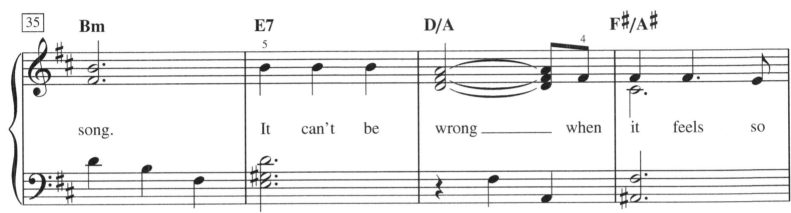

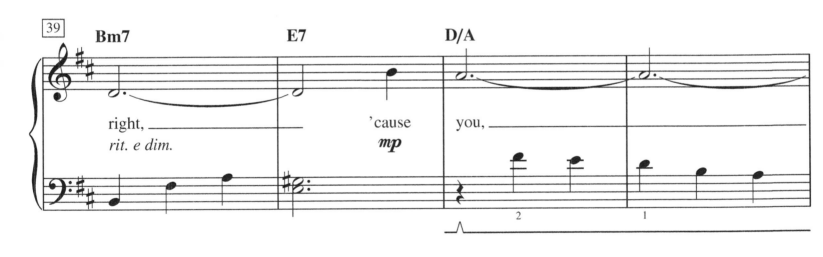

YOU RAISE ME UP

Words and Music by BRENDAN GRAHAM
and ROLF LOVLAND
Arranged by Phillip Keveren

52

YOU'LL NEVER WALK ALONE

from CAROUSEL

Lyrics by OSCAR HAMMERSTEIN II
Music by RICHARD RODGERS
Arranged by Phillip Keveren

With great warmth, like a hymn (♩ = 120-126)

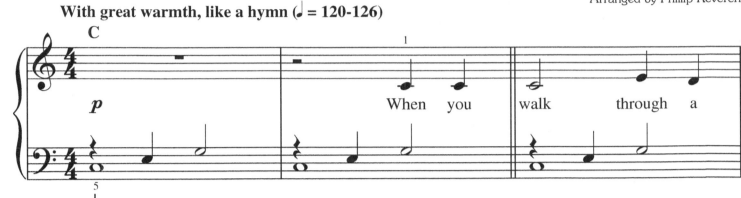

When you walk through a

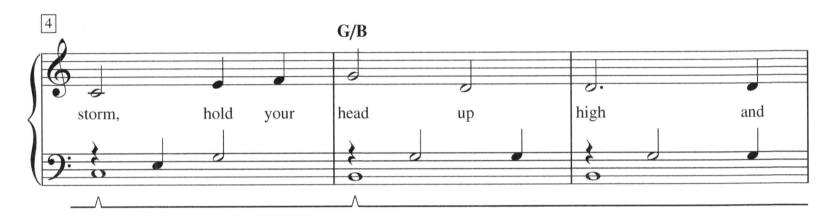

storm, hold your head up high and

don't be a- fraid of the dark.

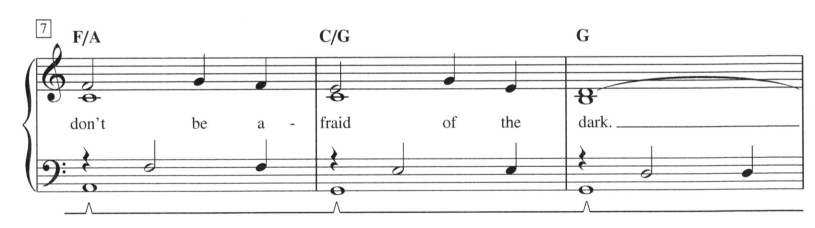

At the end of the storm is a

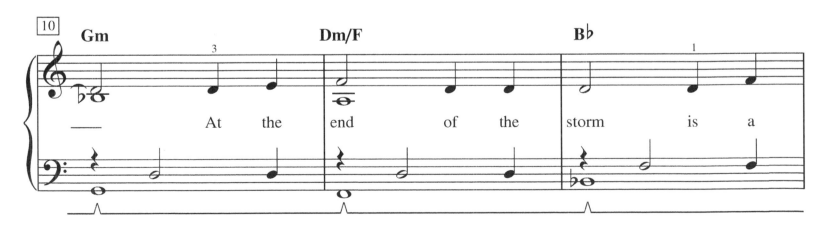

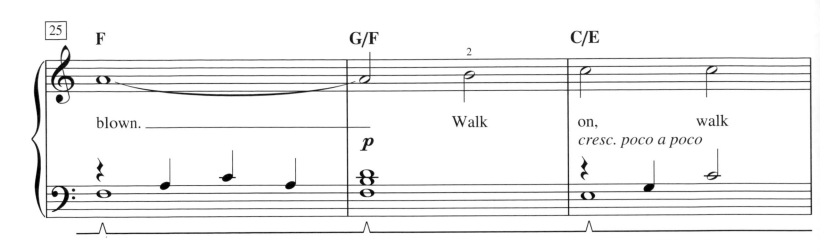

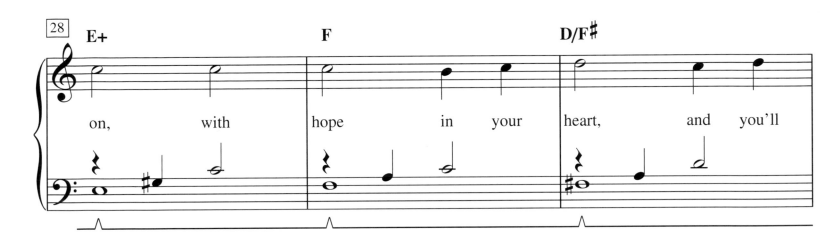

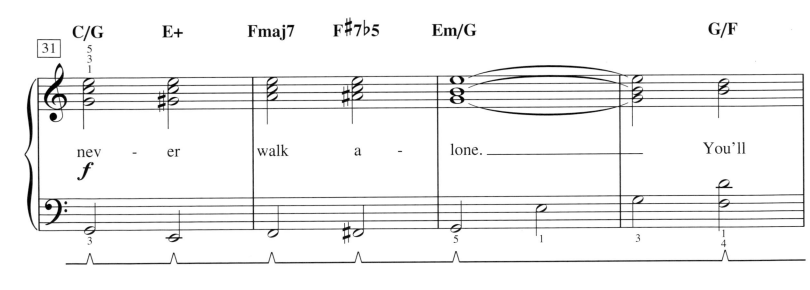

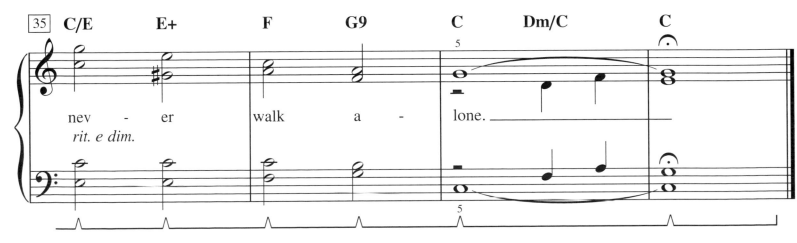